Shakespeare's Insults

for

THE OFFICE

Books by Wayne F. Hill and Cynthia J. Öttchen

SHAKESPEARE'S INSULTS

SHAKESPEARE'S INSULTS FOR DOCTORS

SHAKESPEARE'S INSULTS FOR LAWYERS

SHAKESPEARE'S INSULTS FOR THE OFFICE

SHAKESPEARE'S INSULTS FOR TEACHERS

SHAKESPEARE'S INSULTS

FOR

THE OFFICE

WAYNE F. HILL

AND

CYNTHIA J. ÖTTCHEN

—

ILLUSTRATIONS

BY

TOM LULEVITCH

CLARKSON POTTER/PUBLISHERS
NEW YORK

Published by Clarkson N. Potter/Publishers,
201 East 50th Street, New York, New York 10022.
Member of the Crown Publishing Group.

Random House, Inc.
New York, Toronto, London, Sydney, Auckland

http://randomhouse.com/

CLARKSON N. POTTER, POTTER, and colophon
are trademarks of Clarkson N. Potter, Inc.

Printed in the United States of America

Design by Alexander Knowlton
@ BEST Design Incorporated

Library of Congress Cataloging-in-Publication Data is
available upon request.

ISBN 0-517-70449-8

10 9 8 7 6 5 4 3 2 1

First Edition

This book is dedicated to a pair of old friends who now live on different continents. One illegally diverted $2,000 of his federal student loan to set up a small company and is now a millionaire. Too modest to allow his name to appear in print, he is a typical example of how an education in the liberal arts (certainly he came across Shakespeare somewhere along the line) throws open the door to success. The second much-esteemed friend (who will not be coaxed from anonymity either) unknowingly inspired this work: he decided early in his distinguished career that if he was going to be good he wasn't going to be liked.

What's here? the portrait

of a blinking idiot,

Presenting me a schedule?

THE MERCHANT OF VENICE

CONTENTS

INTRODUCTION

> William Shakespeare is
> often mistaken for
> a playwright or poet,
> but he was actually
> a businessman.
> He managed a company
> that outperformed all
> competitors, earning him
> early retirement with an
> immense personal fortune.

Had he been a writer, he would have strug-
gled desperately to the very end to make
himself more and more famous. But self-
promotion was unimportant to him: the odd
scholar can still doubt he existed at all. No,
Shakespeare was a manager first and fore-

most. Like readers of this book, he and his colleagues worked day in and day out to turn a good penny. His plays are great literature only by coincidence. They not only piled up a fortune for him, but in them he recorded, hidden among the lines and unnoticed until now, his own astonishing formula for success.

"All the world's a stage" is the clue to discovering Shakespeare's secrets within the scraps of writing he left behind. His own stage was a theater named the Globe, open to the sky and built in the round, which he famously referred to as "this wooden O." *O* stands for *officium*—Latin for "office"— which stripped of religious trappings means "get the work done" or just "do it." Shakespeare was four hundred years ahead of his time: All the world's an office.

In the age of the global village, the world keeps getting smaller. Corporate mergers result in ever fewer companies. Electronics reduce the size of even these. Multinational corporations now operate in machines small enough to get lost in a briefcase on the Concorde. Entire continents have moved virtually next door to one another and, oddly enough, seem to get along as well as ever. Which is to say hardly at all. The office is a microcosm of society remaking the world in its own image. Because the office is slimming down, the world has to fit into less and less space.

There is not enough room in the office for anything but the essential aspects of interpersonal relationships. As the language of business is compressed into bits and bytes, so the language of life in the office environment must also be streamlined. Ordinary language spoken during working hours is full of office politics, deadlines, and competition. Everyone is hell-bent on self-assertion, which competes against everyone else's assertions, to pump the maximum volume of human air space full of their own warm and humid mass. These private weather systems ceaselessly collide in storms, frosts, and draughts of offense. For better or worse, the essence of human interaction is *conflict*. And the language of conflict is the *insult*.

When we restrict ourselves to insults, we discover that nothing of consequence is left out. But ordinary insults will never do. Shakespeare's 10,000 insults from his 38 plays are universally sanctioned by cultural and educational authorities worldwide. Voted recently in America the most all-encompassing genius in the history of the human race, the Bard preserves humanity in invective. He arms the discerning to finger human folly.

Loaded with career credibility, Shakespeare's plays contain the new power concept for today's office. Every sort of person in every conceivable situation may be found in an office. All human relationships crowd into its diminishing square footage.

Even that once familiar corporate institution, the office romance, is now a matter of conflict. As all genders gain access to equal power, those heated negotiations over the water cooler and the intramural desk Olympics fall into the very four categories into which we have organized this book: superiors, subordinates, clients, and competitors.

Shakespeare anticipated, as the world and its offices would become smaller, that full-sized, 1:1 scale model human beings could never fit. People would need reduction themselves, and Shakespeare knew how to do it.

And so, his slurs are the next wave of organizational philosophy for the condensed office. Hardly anyone remains convinced for long by shamelessly over-sold incomplete truths—whether reengineering the office, downsizing the organization, managing by objectives, emulating various half-civilized conquerors, or pretending the same old boring analysis has something to do with total quality. Overheated common sense is cooked up by self-styled consultants to make themselves fat with alleged best-sellers and traveling seminars.

Amid the smoke and mirrors of all the management theories and leadership programs, people in the office world have been told how to dress for success, how to network, how to burnish their image—in short, how to compliment. No one until now has told people how to insult effectively. This is a major new direction in management thinking. Whereas compliments take up valuable time (which equals money) and create disgusting companies full of obnoxiously smiling people who fool no one, insults get immediate attention. People have antennae for innuendo.

Management by invective approaches the current office environment as it actually is, venting the hot air, deflating uncompressed egos, and clearing a path to riches and fame.

BOSSES AND EMPLOYEES

You have trained me

like a peasant.

AS YOU LIKE IT
1 . 1 . 68

BOSSES ARE MEANT TO inspire excellence, to be fair, resourceful, respectful, and well-balanced. Their qualities invariably provide a model for common emulation by setting the tone for company gossip. But no one expects the boss to be perfect all the time. For in practice bosses are almost always control freaks, overpaid, exploitative, workaholic, or some combination thereof.

However, everyone but the boss knows that every office is run by everyone but the boss. This time-honored rule is violated only at risk of dire consequences, which fall into three categories: haste, delay, or disillusionment.

If management urges speed, someone might actually finish a project by its drop-dead deadline in such a way that it needn't be redone, thus weighing down the entire office with the unnecessary task of reorganizing for some new achievement. If the boss insists on care, someone will have to block the flush of routine to address tedious questions of quality, forcing the glazed-over office to stare at some unsavory job even a split second longer. Such interference must be avoided at all cost, for the status quo is the foundation upon which employees build their empires. If challenged to justify this foundation, employees will resort to the fall-back option of avoiding reality. This involves claiming to have outgrown youthful idealism and to live now in the "real world." But self-styled disillusionment is only the most stubborn illusion. In short, employees have developed character traits to avoid success, failure, and reality. As every boss knows, and stereotype confirms, the typical employee is disloyal, worthless, incompetent, and lazy.

CONTROL FREAK BOSS

BULLYING IS AN OFFICE SPORT anyone can play. It takes at least two players. The senior one (the boss) pretends to know how he wants business to be conducted; the other needs a paycheck. The only rule is that the second player must stick around for payday.

The control-freak boss gives detailed instructions for every activity, usually just after it has been completed. This is not accidental, for it is essential that every action the subordinate makes be scrutinized and every move corrected. Thus the boss achieves the goal, which is to maintain a creative tension between initiative and error. Initiative is demanded by withholding clear guidance, and error is inevitable as proof (by contrast) of the boss's perfection.

This game is perhaps unique in that only one player is allowed to score. The second player's objective is either to amass an enormous pile of paychecks or to learn the moves as quickly as possible so she can play boss— and get bigger paychecks. In fact, everyone but the most junior person constantly plays both sides, although with different people.

Boss players already assume the right to control every move in every non-boss's life, like a schoolteacher looming over a "bad" child. If they are not being knuckle-rapped or overdosed with instructions by the control freak, they are worked to death by the slave driver. Now subordinates can dust off their dignity, take Shakespeare out of school, and at least mentally put a firm finger on the boss's bad behavior.

In civility thou seem'st so empty.

As You Like It
2. 7. 94

Hear you this Triton of the minnows?

CORIOLANUS

3. 1. 88

While she is here, a man may live as quiet in hell as in a sanctuary, and people sin upon purpose, because they would go thither.

MUCH ADO ABOUT NOTHING
2. 1. 241–43

[His] ambition swell'd so much that it did almost stretch the sides o' th' world.

CYMBELINE
3. 1. 50–52

When he is best, he is a little worse than a man, and when he is worst he is little better than a beast.

THE MERCHANT OF VENICE
1. 2. 83–85

It is certain that when he makes water, his urine is congealed ice.

MEASURE FOR MEASURE
3. 2. 105–7

How tartly that gentleman looks! I never can see him but I am heart-burned an hour after.

MUCH ADO ABOUT NOTHING
2. 1. 3–4

MOST BOSSES ARE IN COMMAND because they are clever enough to get the most money with no connection whatsoever to the work they do. They are paid handsomely for achieving astounding success in their endeavor to convince the company to pay them handsomely.

Exaggerations of this triumph are leaked to the boss's subordinates. The presence of such a legendary business hero in their midst is meant to dissuade them from their own efforts to convince the company to pay them handsomely, an obstacle which the clever ones surmount. And so on.

The successfully overpaid boss is responsible to create barriers for subordinates in order to preserve her own larger piece of the pie. This requires that every comprehensible link between her worth and her pay must be obscured, through one of two techniques. Confusion is one, where the boss may take significant remuneration in perquisites that are easily disguised, so that her salary seems maddeningly proportionate to her work. This drives subordinates, who are totally oriented toward personal financial gain, off the rails.

The second and more impressive approach relies on chaos. The boss is blatantly paid enormous sums, but she feigns madness, ineptitude, foolishness, willful stupidity, violence, moodiness, absence, or any combination of the above. This bold tactic creates an aura around the boss, a hint of the unhinged genius, an impression that something of great value is being missed.

Sophisticated insults can throw such posers off balance just enough to create room to maneuver into the specious realms of overpaid management.

To say nothing, to do nothing, to know
nothing, and to have nothing, is to be
a great part of your title, which is
within a very little of nothing.

ALL'S WELL THAT ENDS WELL
2. 4. 23–26

Thy noble shape is but a form of wax
Digressing from the valour of a man.

ROMEO AND JULIET
3. 3. 125–26

O monstrous beast, how like a swine he lies!

THE TAMING OF THE SHREW
IND. 1. 32

He that trusts to you,
Where he should find you lions,
finds you hares;
Where foxes, geese.

CORIOLANUS
1. 1. 169–71

Fit to govern? No, not to live.

MACBETH
4. 3. 102–3

Thou, which art but air.

THE TEMPEST
5. 1. 21

We think him over-proud
And under-honest, in self-assumption greater
Than in the note of judgement.

TROILUS AND CRESSIDA
2. 3. 125–27

O how vile an idol proves this god!

TWELFTH NIGHT
3. 4. 374

What a sweep of vanity comes this way.

TIMON OF ATHENS

1. 2. 128

Weaker than a woman's tear,
Tamer than sleep, fonder than ignorance,
Less valiant than the virgin in the night,
And skilless as unpractis'd infancy.

TROILUS AND CRESSIDA
1. 1. 9–12

[He is] the best persuaded of himself, so
crammed (as he thinks) with excellencies, that
it is his grounds of faith that all that look on
him love him.

TWELFTH NIGHT
2. 3. 146–52

EXPLOITATIVE BOSS

THE VERY WORD *economic* means getting a lot for a little, passing it off as more than it is, and keeping the change. The ideal combination is low cost, no service, and minimum standards (and those compromised). A relentless profit-chasing attitude drives the proudest commercial achievements. Even luxury goods are merely expensive, as any serious complaint will reveal. "Integrity" is a device for the advertising department. Occasionally a senior person in an office will confuse selling goods or services with satisfying the needs of customers. Business either creates needs or exploits them, and any idea about satisfying needs is sheer sentimentality, is bad for profits, and must be expunged.

Bosses must economize on ideas and concentrate their talents on a single approach— honestly treating their employees just like customers and competitors. The boss would only confuse himself if he did not get the most for the least from everyone in the office. Naturally this means paying busy and highly qualified people such a pittance that they believe they are sufficiently worthless to run personal errands, make coffee, and feed the piranhas without thanks.

The following slurs, however, allow employees, customers, and competitors to use a single approach of their own in dispersing bosslike congregations of vapors.

Who is so gross that cannot
see this palpable device?

RICHARD III
3. 6. 10–11

Pernicious blood-sucker of sleeping men!

HENRY VI, PART 2

3. 2. 4–5

Thy sin's not accidental, but a trade.

MEASURE FOR MEASURE
3. 1. 148

No man's pie is freed from his ambitious finger.

HENRY VIII
1. 1. 52–53

Gold were as good as twenty orators,
And will, no doubt, tempt him to anything.

RICHARD III
4. 2. 38–39

You smell this business with a sense as cold
as is a dead man's nose.

THE WINTER'S TALE
2. 1. 151–52

[You] pedlar's excrement.

THE WINTER'S TALE
4. 4. 713–14

WORKAHOLIC BOSS

THE HEROICALLY DEDICATED manager will treat family and friends just as he treats employees, clients, and competitors. His singlemindedness has an emotional effect closely akin to invective. This is sometimes taken as a personal slight, but it is only a sign of others' lack of imagination.

Workaholism itself is sometimes a form of confusion. Certain bosses create the appearance of constant work when they do very little at all. While practicing golf putts behind closed conference room doors, their constant presence is a reassuring conscience in the office that goads everyone else to ceaseless labor. For some workaholics, the work is other people's. Chosen insults let these other people respond in kind.

Truly thou art damned, like an
ill-roasted egg, all on one side.

As You Like It
3. 2. 36–37

Go forward and be chok'd with thy ambition!

Henry VI, Part 1
2. 4. 112

Thou art a slave, whom Fortune's tender arm
With favour never clasp'd, but bred a dog.

Timon of Athens
4. 3. 252–53

Traffic's thy god, and thy god confound thee!

TIMON OF ATHENS
1. 1. 238

*Thy great fortunes
Are made thy chief afflictions.*

TIMON OF ATHENS
4. 2. 43–44

Live, and love thy misery.

TIMON OF ATHENS
4. 3. 398

DISLOYAL EMPLOYEE

TRADITIONAL MANAGERIAL paranoia properly suspects disloyalty in people merely for having keys to the office and knowing minor company secrets. But there is worse to fear. An employee might actually be faithful —but to something other than securing bonuses for senior management. At very worst, someone in the office might threaten the very underpinnings of commerce by actually caring about life.

Shakespeare created a system for unmasking lukewarm devotion toward work. Insults

You are as a candle, the better part burnt out.

HENRY IV, PART 2

1. 2. 155–56

tinged with wit and humor will cause the
insufficiently serious employee to smile or
even laugh, whereas the loyal employee will
remain stern or take offense. Just as Hamlet
watched his uncle's guilty eyes, so the boss
can flush out the uncommitted by circulat-
ing this book, then pounce upon them with
the following sober-minded phrases.

[Their] constancies
Expire before their fashions.

ALL'S WELL THAT ENDS WELL
1. 2. 62–63

[They are] muddied, thick, and unwholesome
in their thoughts and whispers.

HAMLET
4. 5. 81–82

Seems he a dove? His feathers are but borrow'd,
For he's disposed as the hateful raven:
Is he a lamb? His skin is surely lent him,
For he's inclin'd as is the ravenous wolves.

HENRY VI, PART 2
3. 1. 75–78

With a foul traitor's name stuff I thy throat.

RICHARD II
1. 1. 44

The fiend gives the more friendly counsel.

THE MERCHANT OF VENICE
2. 2. 29

Some that smile have in their hearts, I fear,
millions of mischiefs.

JULIUS CAESAR
4. 1. 50–51

You speak unskillfully: or, if your knowledge
be more, it is much darkened in your malice.

MEASURE FOR MEASURE
3. 2. 142–44

You spotted snakes with double tongue!

A MIDSUMMER NIGHT'S DREAM
2. 2. 9

Snakes, in my heart-blood warm'd,
that sting my heart!

RICHARD II
3. 2. 131

WORKERS' WORK IS MEANT to multiply what it costs to employ them. In the manager's conservative calculations, no employee should receive more than the cumulative expense of his or her screwups, less the value of the pleasure of having him or her around. It works out, then, that most employees should be paid nothing. The rest should pay the company for the privilege of saying they are not unemployed. A few should simply get used to the idea of slavery. The benefits of having a job are more than a paycheck, after all, and overgenerosity is merely inflationary.

Shakespeare obviously liked close calculations, for he has equipped managers and coworkers with words to remind employees of their true monetary worth.

What a coil's here,
Serving of becks and jutting-out of bums!
I doubt whether their legs be worth the sums
That are given for 'em.

TIMON OF ATHENS
1. 2. 232–35

And so from hour to hour, we ripe, and ripe,
And then from hour to hour, we rot, and rot.

As You Like It
2. 7. 26–27

Either you must confess yourselves wondrous
malicious, or be accus'd of folly.

Coriolanus
1. 1. 86–88

We hold our time too precious to be spent
With such a brabbler.

King John #5
2. 161–62

You are not worth the dust which the rude
wind blows in your face.

King Lear
4. 2. 30–31

He swore a thing to me on Monday night,
which he forswore on Tuesday morning.

Much Ado About Nothing
5. 1. 164–66

You rise to play, and go to bed to work.

Othello
2. 1. 115

He hath eaten me out of house and home,
he hath put all my substance into that
fat belly of his.

HENRY IV, PART 2
2. 1. 72–73

INCOMPETENCE IS THE DIFFERENCE between promise and delivery. Naturally, every sensible employee puts his best foot forward when presenting herself to her boss or a client, confident in his ability to come through with excuses and side-step responsibility when things go horribly wrong. The astute employee understands that disasters are always opportunities for the person who caused them to intervene impressively with a bold proposal for fixing the problem, that is, with yet another promise. Self-promotion involves little risk. Best foot forward, side step, best foot forward, side step: this is the dance to the top.

Reliable employees can't dance. They do not draw attention to themselves, and as a result they rarely require pay raises or promotions. As they diligently clean up the messes of their two-stepping colleagues, all the benefit of their labor accrues to the company. Should a small setback blot any of these office stalwarts, the boss will suddenly realize not only that such people exist but how much he has come to rely on them. In the phrase "being taken for granted," the word *granted* means that the boss's expectation is tantamount to a promise from the employee. When reliable employees miscue, the boss finds himself staring dead into the face of flat-footed incompetence. For such a situation the fair and sensitive leader will have a repertoire of emotional invective.

What a past-saving slave is this!

ALL'S WELL THAT ENDS WELL
4. 3. 135

Cudgel thy brains no more about it, for your dull ass will not mend his pace with beating.

HAMLET
5. 1. 56—57

I have seen small reflection of her wit.

CYMBELINE
1. 3. 29—30

In human action and capacity,
[they are] of no more soul nor
fitness for the world than camels.

CORIOLANUS
2. 1. 247—49

Throw this slave upon the dunghill.

KING LEAR

3. 7. 95–96

[He was] a fool, an empty purse,
There was no money in't: not Hercules
Could have knock'd out his brains,
for he had none.

4. 2. 113–15

Canst thou believe thy living is a life,
So stinkingly depending? Go mend, go mend.

MEASURE FOR MEASURE
3. 2. 25–26

Mere prattle without practice.

OTHELLO
1. 1. 26

The cur is excellent at faults.

TWELFTH NIGHT
2. 5. 128–29

Thou half-penny purse of wit,
thou pigeon-egg of discretion.

LOVE'S LABOUR'S LOST
5. 1. 69–70

Thou art too base to be a acknowledg'd.

THE WINTER'S TALE
4. 4. 419–20

SOME EMPLOYEES IMAGINE that they have lives beyond the confines of the office. This illusion fills their heads with ideas of self-worth that distract them from the pleasures of meeting deadlines and achieving company objectives.

The shorthand synonym for this life of the mind is "laziness." Most lazy employees are quick enough to take that personal telephone call, rush out to lunch, or leave early. They are pioneering a fashionable new style of career planning that elegantly avoids anything so presumptuous as an actual goal. Aware that the world is shrinking, they base their plans on the sophisticated concept of keeping themselves from disappearing. So-called lazy people are working hard to take offense at any claim upon their energies. Their pace at work is actually heroic resistance against digitization, and occasionally even heroes need their rest.

At the root of their philosophy lies a conviction that the world owes them something.

Idle weeds are fast in growth.

RICHARD III
3. 1. 103

The informed boss (or coworker or client)
can now give it to them verbally.

I should take you for idleness itself.

ANTONY AND CLEOPATRA
1. 3. 92–93

'Tis sweating labour,
To bear such idleness so near the heart.

ANTONY AND CLEOPATRA
1. 3. 93–94

I abhor this dilatory sloth.

HENRY VIII
2. 4. 234–35

I have seen drunkards do more
than this in sport.

KING LEAR
2. 1. 35–36

Tardy sluggard.

RICHARD III
5. 3. 226

How now, you whoreson peasant,
Where have you been these two days loitering?

THE TWO GENTLEMEN OF VERONA
4. 4. 43–44

CLIENTS AND THE COMPETITION

I think thee now some

common customer.

ALL'S WELL THAT END'S WELL
5. 3. 280

A CUSTOMER, OR CLIENT, is a person who cannot be bothered to do what he wants, but instead wants you to do it for him. He fully justifies your state-of-the-art billing system, and makes producing your goods or services almost worth the trouble.

Clients ultimately pay everyone's salary or wages and fund all the benefits and per-quisites that make office life so gratifying. But not satisfied with the sales force's servile fawning, subtle flattery, and epic promises, many clients who might otherwise pass for well-adjusted egomaniacs sincerely believe they run your office. They do not.

Clients are responsible for filling order books without dithering, signing contracts without the discourtesy of reading fine print, paying bills instantaneously, and tak-ing what's delivered without stirring up the legal community. Customers have a right to demand fine vintage smarm, but they need to be curbed from dictating policy or setting standards.

On the other hand, the competition has the right to lust after your apparent success. Their dreams of total wealth and power must not be encroached upon by anyone else's fictions, for what threatens fantasy is not reality but another fantasy. The public imagination (the media) is terrified by the one idea that restricts the exclusive right of every individual to his own vices: the hated word *monopoly.*

Monopoly is so widely feared that when no one else could possibly care less about what some office somewhere does, it becomes vitally important to invent competition. Law requires it. If no one steps forward, the government itself must intervene in the national interest and subsidize a rival.

With this single exception, in which competition is a public service, akin to the twin benefits of conscription and tax collection, any office's competitors are always arrogant and unscrupulous. Arrogance (that is, disguised inferiority) and unscrupulousness are extremely attractive qualities—for Shakespeare's invective.

TIME-WASTING CLIENTS

A PRINCIPAL OBJECT OF office work is to accommodate people who have no idea what they want. Dealing with such individuals risks burning up one's own generous resources of patience and goodwill, not to mention good humor.

The solution is to act like an answering machine. When the telephone rings, relax, carry on pretending to do other work, pick up the receiver, and, despite anything the caller attempts to say, chime in with any of the following insults. The caller will not notice anything unusual. Repeat them at will for that expensive system effect, beep, and go silent. Should you hear anything remotely interesting, you may switch back to the admittedly inferior "human" mode and apologize for having been away at an important meeting. Talented members of the office staff will soon learn to achieve the same impressive time-saving results in person as on the telephone.

Be better employed, and be naught awhile.

AS YOU LIKE IT
1. 1. 34–35

*More of your conversation would
infect my brain.*

CORIOLANUS
2. 1. 93–94

[Here's] one who the music of
his own vain tongue
Doth ravish like enchanting harmony.

LOVE'S LABOUR'S LOST
1. 1. 165–66

[You] speak an infinite deal of nothing.

THE MERCHANT OF VENICE
1. 1. 113

[You are] duller than a great thaw.

MUCH ADO ABOUT NOTHING
2. 1. 228

Thou thing of no bowels thou!

TROILUS AND CRESSIDA
2. 1. 52

[You are] a feather for each wind that blows.

THE WINTER'S TALE
2. 3. 153

FORMERLY NOTORIOUS CLIENTS are suddenly having greatness thrust upon them. The cheapskate who chronically fails to pay bills on time is emerging as the exemplar of a new management trend. As offices have downsized, economic conditions conspire to render everything superfluous, including profit.

Succeeding in the profitless office is uncharted territory for many nervous managers. They can turn for guidance, however, to the long experience of other previously underappreciated players, whose expertise gains new importance. These experts, who are easy to locate at the top of the debtors list, have learned to make the ceaseless business of doing business its own reward. Theoretically, with the profit motive out of the question, there is no longer a strict economic need for parsimony, and, in practice, these managers' favored characteristic of being cheap purely for cheapness's sake has come into its own.

A friendly visit to such a client's office,

whether or not accompanied by accountants and the police, will reveal that the boss's personal involvement has a crucial effect in the profitless office. Low wages and paltry benefits are favorite methods of expressing his characteristic trait. In particularly creative cases the effect is magnified by contrast with the boss's own pay and benefits. But other noticeable measures have perhaps a more immediate effect on the morale of the office work force. Patched-up equipment, bone-aching furniture, plastic plants, short supplies of inferior paper that keeps jamming an off-brand copy machine, and, as a final touch, rationed toilet tissue all successfully reassure the office of their boss's leadership and make coming to work a bracing experience. With greatness comes respect. The boss who claims that pulling together as a team, and extended credit terms, are necessary because he's broke, deserves the following expressions of admiration.

His coffers sound
With hollow poverty and emptiness.

HENRY IV, PART 2
1. 3. 74–75

I know a discontented gentleman,
Whose humble means match not his
haughty spirit.

RICHARD III

4. 2. 36–37

He's poor, and that's revenge enough.

TIMON OF ATHENS

3. 4. 62–63

Words pay no debts.

TROILUS AND CRESSIDA

3. 2. 55

*These debts may well be call'd desperate ones,
for a madman owes 'em.*

TIMON OF ATHENS

3. 4. 100–1

*Our business is become a nullity,
Yea, and a woeful and a piteous nullity.*

THE TWO NOBLE KINSMEN

3. 5. 51–52

LITIGIOUS CLIENTS

TOO FREQUENTLY, HYPERSENSITIVE clients or customers will choose to involve professional complainers in the process of making illegitimate claims or extorting adjustments. Lawyers, as these people sometimes call themselves, contribute little except to bring into the august setting of a public courtroom the flash and spectacle of a fire-sale bazaar. Such undignified action abuses the sterling intentions of companies everywhere, dedicated as they invariably are to serving humanity and maintaining high standards.

Very occasionally a responsible company will ask other lawyers to point out the presumptuousness of the litigant's assumptions and suggest the venality of his intentions. In this generosity of spirit, a client's attorneys deserve no lower standard of insults than the members of one's own office.

The gold I give thee will I melt and pour
Down thy ill-uttering throat.

ANTONY AND CLEOPATRA
2. 5. 34–35

Could I come near your beauty with my nails
I'd set my ten commandments in your face.

HENRY VI, PART 2
1. 3. 141–42

Their tongues rot that speak against us!

ANTONY AND CLEOPATRA
3. 7. 15–16

*Do thy best to pluck this crawling
serpent from my breast!*

**A MIDSUMMER NIGHT'S DREAM
2. 2. 144–45**

Hath not Fortune sent in this fool
to cut off the argument?

AS YOU LIKE IT
1. 2. 44–45

The complaints I have heard of you I do not
all believe; 'tis my slowness that I do not;
for I know you lack not folly to commit them
and have ability enough to make
such knaveries yours.

ALL'S WELL THAT ENDS WELL
1. 3. 8–11

His gift is in devising impossible slanders.

MUCH ADO ABOUT NOTHING
2. 1. 128

UNSCRUPULOUS COMPETITION

THERE IS A SIMPLE TRUTH at the heart
of normal business practice. Any other firm
with a concept similar to yours obviously
engages in corporate espionage. There is no
need to investigate further. Not only have
they stolen your idea, but every client they
attract is another proof that they have
mounted a campaign to discredit you and

wreck your long and distinguished profit record. The only ethical solution is to steal their secrets, while creating a new line of inferior products yourself and advertising them so heavily that your rivals will soon copy them with products that are worse yet.

Without sullying your reputation by making any improvements to your services or products, you divert your detractors. Without recriminations or lawsuits, which would merely serve to encourage your rivals and give them satisfaction, you regain your ascendancy. The risk is that your next advertising campaign to relaunch your old ordinary products as "new and improved" may not succeed. The public may have developed a libido for the banal, worthless, and ugly. If that does occur, all is not lost, for you can then reassert your own superiority through the quality of your invective.

If he were honester he were much goodlier.

ALL'S WELL THAT ENDS WELL
3. 5. 79–80

He would pawn his fortunes to hopeless
restitution, so he might be called
your vanquisher.

CORIOLANUS
3. 1. 15–17

One may smile, and smile, and be a villain.

HAMLET
1. 5. 108

If I be served such another trick, I'll have my
brains ta'en out and buttered, and give them
to a dog for a New Year's gift.

THE MERRY WIVES OF WINDSOR
3. 5. 6–8

These are the forgeries of jealousy.

A MIDSUMMER NIGHT'S DREAM
2. 1. 81

Have I laid my brain in the sun and dried it,
that it wants matter to prevent so gross o'er-
reaching as this? 'Tis time I were choked with
a piece of toasted cheese.

THE MERRY WIVES OF WINDSOR
5. 5. 136–40

[You are] thieves unworthy
of a thing so stol'n.

TROILUS AND CRESSIDA
2. 2. 95

Thou art baser than a cutpurse.

THE TWO NOBLE KINSMEN
2. 2. 213

This place is famous for the creatures of prey
that keep upon't.

THE WINTER'S TALE
3. 3. 12–13

It is fit I should commit offense to my inferiors.

CYMBELINE
2. 1. 30–31

OFFICE RITUALS

How courtesy would seem

to cover sin!

PERICLES, PRINCE OF TYRE
1. 1. 122

LIKE LITTLE RELIGIONS, offices thrive on ritual. Initiates endure a series of labors until they attain a state of modest incompetence, in which they retire in place and set about the task of obstructing change. Junior workers are always distrusted (depraved by the original sins of youth and imagination) and would only waste their time if they behaved in any corporate-spirited way, which is why they do not.

It is with ambition and necessity that the company courtesies emerge. These begin with the art of inflating the self-importance of anyone who could possibly influence one's own success. This sycophancy is followed immediately by mastering the science of meetings. By and large this art and this science are the only required skills for a notable office career. All that remain are the minor specialist rigors connected with appeasing government officials or ignoring the press.

There is one further exertion, although it is rarely used. Because, for dubious legal reasons, companies must be able to prove that their devotees are not actually slaves but voluntarily endure bizarre hardships without

threat or compulsion (not to mention indoc-
trination), there is a final ritual—quitting.

BUTTERING UP

THE SUPREME BENEFIT of attaining
power is that one can cease to be encum-
bered with reality. Hopeful people sur-
rounding the "Great One" stop bothering
him or her with truth. Instead they massage
the deserving ego with inventive ideas of
what they think the leader wants to hear.
Thus, power stimulates creativity. And creativity is the lifeblood of any office striving to
keep up with the times.

Although flattery, strictly speaking, might
not be the original invention of anyone now
living, its present application elevates mer-
chants to the former level of kings, a number
of whom lent their names to Shakespeare's
works. The mere sound of Shakespearean
language has a flattering effect on many of
those who have transcended the need to
hear what is being said. But the Bard arms
the rare honest individual to stir up the
emperor's whole naked court with mutter-
ings about flatterers themselves.

Here comes a flattering rascal.

CYMBELINE
1. 6. 27

*When I tell him he hates flatterers, he says he
does, being then most flattered.*

JULIUS CAESAR
2. 1. 207–8

*They praise you, and make an ass of you.
Now your foes tell you plainly you are
an ass: so that by your foes, sir, you
profit in the knowledge of yourself,
and by your friends you are abused.*

TWELFTH NIGHT
5. 1. 16–19

*A subtle slippery knave, a finder
out of occasions; that has an eye can
stamp and counterfeit the true advantages
never present themselves!*

OTHELLO
2. 1. 240–42

O heavy ignorance, that praises the worst best.

OTHELLO
2. 1. 143

What a candy deal of courtesy
This fawning greyhound then did proffer me!

HENRY IV, PART I
1. 3. 247–48

I never heard such a drawling,
affecting rogue.

THE MERRY WIVES OF WINDSOR
2. 1. 137

[You] attended to their sugar'd words,
But look'd not on the poison of their hearts.

RICHARD III
3. 1. 13–14

O calm, dishonourable, vile submission.

ROMEO AND JULIET
3. 1. 72

He that loves to be flattered is
worthy o' th' flatterer.

TIMON OF ATHENS
1. 1. 225–26

Glass-fac'd flatterer.

TIMON OF ATHENS
1. 1. 59

Let the candied tongue lick absurd pomp.

HAMLET
3. 2. 60

MEETINGS ARE THE principal product of nearly every company. They play the essential role of preventing rash action, but they must be carefully controlled. When rival factions gather to parade their attainments and shame the opposition, the discussion may accidentally wander down paths that could lead to decision and even implementation. This must be avoided, for innovation in one area invariably affects another.

Meetings must follow rules. It has been written that no project should be initiated until everyone is convinced that it ought to be done, and has been convinced for so long that it is now time to do something else. To allow this cycle its free run, issues must be framed so they can be addressed only by absent experts. For instance, all matters of office politics must be reserved for the judgment of a management consultant who can determine that, wrong or right, every action which is not customary is a dangerous precedent and advise that nothing should ever be done for the first time. Because not everyone agrees that some procedure needs improvement, the only reasonable course of action is to form a committee to report on whether it should be expounded upon further. In fact, these views are deeply indebted to Professor Francis Cornford in his sagacious *Microcosmographia Academica*.

While such essential preliminaries are attended to, the creative momentum vital in effective meetings can be sustained by liberal use of personal remarks from Shakespeare. The following insults are so adaptable that they can constitute an entire meeting in themselves. By arranging them in different sequences, they can actually *be* meetings on nearly any topic.

You lay out too much pains for
purchasing but trouble.

CYMBELINE
2. 3. 88–89

[He is] a gentleman that loves to hear himself
talk, and will speak more in a minute than
he will stand to in a month.

ROMEO AND JULIET
2. 4. 144–46

'Tis such stuff as madmen tongue,
and brain not.

CYMBELINE
5. 4. 146–47

If you be mad, be gone:
if you have reason, be brief.

TWELFTH NIGHT
1. 5. 200–1

O, there has been much throwing
about of brains.

HAMLET
2. 2. 356

It would discredit the blest gods, proud man,
To answer such a question.

TROILUS AND CRESSIDA
4. 5. 246–47

I muse you make so slight a question.

HENRY IV, PART 2
4. 1. 167

Base slave, thy words are blunt,
and so art thou.

HENRY VI, PART 2
4. 1. 67

What mutter you?

HENRY VI, PART 3
1. 1. 169

By heaven, brat, I'll plague ye for that word.

HENRY VI, PART 3
5. 5. 27

We coldly pause for thee.

KING JOHN
2. 1. 53

Confusion now hath made his masterpiece!

MACBETH
2. 3. 67

Thou but offend'st thy lungs to speak so loud.

THE MERCHANT OF VENICE
4. 1. 140

I can see yet without spectacles, and I see no such matter.

MUCH ADO ABOUT NOTHING
1. 1. 176–77

In a false quarrel there is no true valour.

MUCH ADO ABOUT NOTHING
5. 1. 120

*You cram these words into mine ears against
the stomach of my sense.*

THE TEMPEST
2. 1. 102–3

More matter with less art.

HAMLET

2. 2. 94

This bald unjointed chat of his!

HENRY IV, PART I

1. 3. 64

*By this hand, I will supplant
some of your teeth.*

THE TEMPEST

3. 2. 47–48

I profit not by thy talk.

TROILUS AND CRESSIDA

5. 1. 13

Leave thy vain bibble babble.

TWELFTH NIGHT

4. 2. 100

ASSUAGING THE LAW

BY DEFINITION government regulation is disrespectful of everyone in the office. It presumes to doubt the sincerity of people in commerce to behave honestly and questions their commitment to providing humanity with vital goods and services. Conversely, any form of enterprise involves risk, which offends the sensibilities of many government workers. There can be only mutual suspicion. A state of hostility persists. Little has been done to break the impasse, until now.

We have worked out a formula that enables such long-standing antagonists to meet on common ground and exchange views in a mutually accessible language. Both parties are invited to share the same resources—those presented in this book. This ingenious approach enables all factions in any dispute to come to the conference table, which is the objective of much of the world's most notable diplomacy.

You filthy famished correctioner.

HENRY IV, PART 2
5. 4. 21

Get thee glass eyes; and, like a scurvy politician, seem to see the things thou dost not.

KING LEAR
4. 6. 172–74

Vexation almost stops my breath.

HENRY VI, PART 1
4. 3. 41

[You] busy meddling fiend.

HENRY VI, PART 2
3. 3. 21

The first thing we do, let's kill all the lawyers.

HENRY VI, PART 2
4. 2. 73

What sneaking fellow comes yonder?

TROILUS AND CRESSIDA
1. 2. 229

QUITTING

THE EXPENSE OF SPIRIT in an office is addictive. Once a person "belongs," the habit keeps him showing up at nine o'clock every morning year after year. But when the old boy network shows signs of unraveling and glass ceilings fail to exclude the worthy, when automatic privilege becomes ever so slightly conditional, it is time for a person to reconsider his options. Although the old code of lifetime loyalty to a single firm rewards one with a sense of well-being and moral superiority, some rather foolhardy individuals have taken their futures in their own hands and quit.

The fact that some people have survived such impetuosity, and some have even prospered, is no excuse for presuming to live outside the microcosm. Only one justification for this rashness is possible. The agonies of withdrawal from the corporate womb can be worth it for the sheer pleasure of voicing a subtle parting insult.

Descend to darkness and the burning lake.

HENRY VI, PART 2
1 . 4 . 38

I must discontinue your company.

MUCH ADO ABOUT NOTHING
5 . 1 . 186–87

I have too long borne
Your blunt upbraidings and your bitter scoffs.

RICHARD III
1 . 3 . 103–4

Thou art so leaky we must leave thee
to thy sinking.

ANTONY AND CLEOPATRA
3. 13. 63–64

Were all the wealth I have shut up in thee,
I'd give thee leave to hang it.

TIMON OF ATHENS
4. 3. 281–82

We know each other well.
We do, and long to know each other worse.

TROILUS AND CRESSIDA
4. 1. 31–32

Go rot!

THE WINTER'S TALE
1. 2. 324

CONCLUSION

A friend of ours many years ago worked in an office renowned for its unremitting pace. He had an extremely quick mind and soon came to recognize that a certain quality of culture, an indescribable touch of humanity, had been overlooked in formulating the company's goals. However, he seemed to thrive in the office and gained many valuable skills. For instance, he mastered the lawful use of a photocopy machine, which he might never have done, as he was a university graduate. Because the copy center was in the basement, he also learned to navigate with precision in windowless corridors and discovered a talent for near perfect accuracy in operating high-speed elevators.

Working late one evening, he was sent on a desperate copying job by a young project manager who was prematurely gray and unaccountably balding. Sensing the urgency in his manager's face, which was growing permanently lined and distorted by stress, our friend instantly assessed the situation and set off laden with originals.

The full story came to us much later through a chance meeting with a woman who had joined the firm more than two years after these legendary events. The copies failed to appear with our friend's usual speed. Half an hour passed before the rapidly aging young boss returned his attention to the needed copies. A colleague was dispatched in search, only to find the copy center locked and dark.

Our friend had set out and simply kept going, never to return. He is now a celebrated artist and, strange but true, a very highly paid senior troubleshooter in one of America's most colorful skyscraper window washing firms. In the end the unmade copies made no difference whatever, but the point is that the company lost a promising talent.

In contrast, rather than forcing creative people to operate outside, Shakespeare offers a vision of reducing the office, in keeping with the times. But rather than traveling inconvenient distances weighed down with paperwork on a mission to create more, he enables us in human terms to call up whole worlds in a word. The Bard is good value: he gives more with less.